RETIREMENT *for Beginners*

RETIREMENT

for Beginners

RETIREMENT FOR BEGINNERS

An Hachette UK Company
www.hachette.co.uk

Summersdale Publishers Ltd
Part of Octopus Publishing Group Limited
Carmelite House
50 Victoria Embankment
LONDON
EC4Y 0DZ
UK

www.summersdale.com

Printed and bound in Malta

ISBN: 978-1-84953-751-3

Substantial discounts on bulk quantities of Summersdale books are available to corporations, professional associations and other organisations. For details contact general enquiries: telephone: +44 (0) 1243 771107 or email: enquiries@summersdale.com.

RETIREMENT

for Beginners

CLIVE WHICHELOW

summersdale

INTRODUCTION

After all those years of routine you're suddenly free! You're bound to be a bit nervous – it is your first time. No more being bossed about – well, apart from by your other half, of course. No more getting up at the crack of dawn to go to work though at your age you may have to get up at the crack of dawn anyway to use the loo. No more wage slavery – er, no more wages...

But it's going to be fine, because you can now do what you want to do – within reason, naturally. Your chances of becoming a Premier League footballer or supermodel may now be slim – definitely slimmer than you – but look at all those not-so-young people treading the red carpet at the Oscars: Dame Helen, Sir Sean, Sir Anthony...

But back to planet earth for a moment. Retirement is the new work.

We have an ageing population and the number of retired people is growing every year. Before long we'll have about half a dozen school-leavers working round the clock to pay the pensions of 60 million retirees. Well, it serves them right after we subsidised their education for all those years.

The future won't be catwalks strutted by supermodels, but catwalks strutted by superannuated models. The Premier League won't be full of overpaid footballers, but overaged footballers. The YMCA will become the OMCA, and instead of New Kids on the Block it'll be Old Gits on a Pension.

The future is ours – let's enjoy it!

WHAT IS A RETIREE?

It's someone who doesn't work – apart from all the shopping, gardening, housework, DIY, volunteering, family tree research, and all the other things they didn't have time for when they were working. It's someone who still doesn't have a spare minute in the day

It's someone who, after a lifetime of vast acquired knowledge, now spends their days doing wordsearch and sudoku puzzles

It's someone who laughs in the face of bad weather reports, bad traffic reports, glass ceilings and pay freezes

It's someone who is finally getting something back from the government

WHAT IS
RETIREMENT?

Freedom without responsibility

A long holiday without actually
going anywhere

If school was the starter and work was the
main course, this is the dessert – sweet,
self-indulgent and a little bit naughty

The rest of your life

WHAT ARE
THE HOURS?

Unlike a working person, you never clock
off so you'll be permanently available
for any 'little job' your other half or
your offspring can think up for you

You're now on permanent flexitime
so tea breaks and lunchtimes are
whenever the hell you decide they
are – power to the people!

Seeing as you are now a retiree 24/7,
shouldn't you be paid a bit more?
You make junior doctors look like slackers

WHAT'S THE PAY LIKE?

Well, seeing as you're being paid by the government you should be considered a public-sector worker and therefore enjoy a healthy salary with all the perks. But for some reason it doesn't quite work like that

OK, there's a winter fuel allowance, but shouldn't there be a boiled sweet/ mint humbug allowance, or perhaps free membership of the National Trust?

Let's face it, if anyone advertised a job with this salary, no one in their right mind would take it

WHAT DO I HAVE TO DO?

Nothing. Which is actually
quite hard. Before you know it
you'll be extremely busy

Treat every day like a holiday –
though perhaps without the all-night
clubbing and skinny-dipping

Enjoy yourself! Get your money's
worth out of that free bus pass!

Don't tell everyone you're retired or you'll
be lumbered with all sorts of boring/
unpleasant jobs that they don't want to do

THINGS YOU SHOULDN'T BE DOING NOW

Setting the alarm. Unfortunately,
your body clock has been programmed
to wake you up at the same time
every morning anyway

Wondering if you'll get a pay rise this year

Wondering if your old employer is
managing to keep going without you

Going back to your old workplace
when you run out of biros or need
to get a bit of photocopying done

THINGS YOU MIGHT MISS

Phoning in sick

Playing Solitaire on the office computer

Having a boss to moan about

All the gossip

THINGS YOU WON'T MISS

Forking out for endless collections of
birthdays, weddings, people leaving, etc.

The mind-numbing boredom of trying
to look busy when you're not

Having to go out in the morning
when it's still dark

All the gossip about you

LONG-PLANNED RETIREMENT PROJECTS – AND THE REALITY (PART ONE)

PROJECT

To finally read some of the 'classics'

REALITY

Get to page 72 of a *Harry Potter* book

PROJECT

To learn a musical instrument

REALITY

Achieve a shaky 'Chopsticks'
on an electronic keyboard

ODD THINGS THAT WILL HAPPEN

You'll forget when it's the weekend

You'll occasionally have the strange feeling that there's something very important you should be doing – don't worry, there's not!

You'll get unduly excited about it being dustbin day or when the meter reader calls

WIT AND WISDOM YOU WILL ACQUIRE

I don't know how I found
the time to go to work

If I need a rest I'll have to go back to work!

Computers are a complete
mystery to me now

The only thing I miss is the people

Retirement is wasted on the old!

WAYS TO AVOID BEING GIVEN TASKS BY YOUR SPOUSE

Find a time-consuming hobby that gets you out of the house e.g. building up a vast collection of vintage china or visiting every station on the train network

Get a sick note from the doctor – it'll be just like old times!

Insist that it's now illegal under European law to work during retirement

WAYS IN WHICH TO SMOOTH THE TRANSITION

Hold a daily meeting with your other half and talk in silly jargon

Have a small stock of stationery for doodling, rubber-band flicking, ruler twanging, etc.

Spend the first half-hour of each day talking about the previous night's TV

LONG-PLANNED RETIREMENT PROJECTS – AND THE REALITY (PART TWO)

PROJECT

To look up some distant relatives

REALITY

Check their Facebook pages

PROJECT

To run a marathon

REALITY

To run a mile when someone
actually suggests it

PROJECT
To travel to exotic countries like Iceland

REALITY
Go to Iceland for your sausages

CONVERSATIONS YOU WILL NO LONGER HAVE

The nightmares of the one-way
system during the rush hour

The ridiculous cost of your
lunchtime panini

The constant changes in the
company's computer system

Pleading with your boss for a pay rise

CONVERSATIONS YOU MIGHT START HAVING

The nightmares of the queuing
system in your local post office

The ridiculous cost of lunch in
a popular visitor attraction

The constant changes in the
state pension rules

Pleading with the chancellor
of the exchequer for a pension
rise – good luck with that!

THINGS YOU NO LONGER HAVE TO FEEL GUILTY ABOUT

Oversleeping. Though 3 p.m.
may be pushing it a bit

Sitting around doing nothing.
Unless the house is on fire, of course

Putting on a bit of weight. Though
perhaps draw the line if you start
to need reinforced floorboards

PEOPLE WHO MAY NOW EYE YOU WITH SUSPICION

Those poor so-and-sos who still
have to work for a living

Everyone who has to pay exorbitant
public transport costs

Everyone who sees you getting
discounted admission to everything

THINGS TO AVOID SAYING TO FRIENDS WHO ARE STILL WORKING

There's nothing like a little nap after lunch

The supermarket's so lovely and quiet in the week before 10 a.m.

Would you like to buy a second-hand alarm clock?

WHAT RETIREMENT SHOULDN'T BE

Boring

An excuse to take full advantage of
your local pub's all-day opening hours

An excuse to blow your entire
pension pot on a luxury holiday

HOW YOU WILL NOW BE VIEWED BY YOUR WORKING FRIENDS

As a skiver

As someone who can walk their dog for them during the week

As someone who is shamelessly wasting taxpayers' money on enjoying themselves

HOW TO SPOT FELLOW RETIREES

They're the only other people in the
cinema on a Tuesday afternoon

They're the ones who single-handedly
run every charity shop in the country

They travel just one stop on
the bus because it's free

HOW THINGS WILL CHANGE

THEN – AT WORK

Moaning about the filthy temper,
lack of understanding and general
meanness of your boss

NOW – AT HOME

Moaning about the filthy temper,
lack of understanding and general
meanness of your other half

THEN – AT WORK
Watching the clock till going-home time

NOW – AT HOME
Watching the clock till it's not too
early to have a sneaky drink

THEN – AT WORK
Having to look busy when you're not

NOW – AT HOME
Having to look busy when you're not

THEN – AT WORK

Jumping out of bed when the alarm sounds

NOW – AT HOME

Ceremonially burying the
alarm clock in the garden

THINGS YOU CAN NOW DO

Have long, leisurely lunches
without interruption – unless
your spouse is also retired

Finally get your CD and book
collections into alphabetical order

Find 101 different ways of doing nothing

PURSUITS FOR BORED RETIREES (PART ONE)

A) Tot up how much money you earned over the course of your working life

B) Now work out where the hell it's all gone

HOW THINGS HAVE CHANGED

THEN – AT WORK

A chat with your workmates

NOW – AT HOME

A one-to-one with the budgie

THEN – AT WORK
Dissecting last night's TV

NOW – AT HOME
Watching daytime TV

THEN – AT WORK
Shopping in your lunch break

NOW – AT HOME
Having a lunch break in your shopping

THEN – AT WORK
Having a booze-up every time
someone left the company

NOW – AT HOME
Finding a good excuse for a booze-up
whenever you can

THEN – AT WORK
Wondering if the phone
will ever stop ringing

NOW – AT HOME
Checking the phone to see
if it's still working

THINGS YOU SHOULD NOW COMPLAIN ABOUT

Your state pension – obviously!

You're now a sitting duck for cold callers, junk mailers, doorstep salesmen and other assorted nuisances

The fact that just when you got really good at your job you weren't allowed to do it any more

THINGS YOU PROBABLY SHOULDN'T COMPLAIN ABOUT

Being spoilt for choice about
what to do today

Finding all the shops, cafes and garden
centres cluttered up with other retirees

That bank holidays don't feel
special any more – every day
is a holiday for you now!

TRUTHS THAT WILL SLOWLY DAWN ON YOU

You won't get invited to all those office Christmas parties, leaving dos and other jollies

The exorbitant cost of buying your own stationery

You're now extremely unlikely to find yourself on *The Sunday Times* Rich List

FAMOUS PEOPLE WHO CARRIED ON WORKING AFTER 65

Winston Churchill – already 65 when he became a wartime prime minister

—————— ✦ ——————

Ella Fitzgerald – still singing at the age of 75

—————— ✦ ——————

Kirk Douglas – starred in the film *Empire State Building Murders* at the age of 91

——————✕——————

And you're retired – you lazy young whippersnapper, you!

MYSTERIES OF RETIREMENT (PART ONE)

Why would you suddenly want to play golf when it's never occurred to you to do so in the previous sixty-odd years?

Why are retirees often given clocks just when they don't need them any more?

Before you retire, do you simply 'tire'?

OTHER WAYS TO DESCRIBE YOURSELF

Permanently between jobs

Pension consultant

A 'resting' worker

FANTASY INTERLUDE

Did you know that the number
of people of retirement age in the
UK (ten million) is larger than the
population of Sweden (nine million)?

＊

Why, then, don't Britain's retirees form
their own country and have a nice,
quiet life? Imagine… no commuters, no
traffic jams, no boring business news…

＊

No businessmen cluttering up lunchtime
pubs and restaurants… Golf courses
free of people yapping into their
mobile phones or 'clinching deals'…

＊

Bliss!

NEW DEFINITIONS YOU MAY NEED

Working lunch – eating a sandwich while doing the crossword

Annual holiday entitlement – 52 weeks

Business meeting – discussing the paper bill with your newsagent

Hot-desking – moving your cuppa from the kitchen table to the coffee table

THINGS YOU CAN DO NOW THAT YOU COULDN'T BEFORE

Watch an entire TV box set back-to-back

Enjoy a siesta

Catch junk mailers red-handed and give them their flipping pizza leaflets back

Spend the whole day in your dressing gown and slippers

YOUR NEW RESPONSIBILITIES

To keep a straight face while friends
are moaning about their jobs

To become a conversational expert
on all things weather-related

To use your new status to grab as
many discounts as you can

WAYS TO SUPPLEMENT YOUR PENSION

Sell off all your old work clothes

Become a nude artist's model (this might
be essential after the above option)

Hire yourself out as a human satnav
and offer all the traffic-avoidance
tricks you've learnt over the years

EXPERT PENSION ADVICE YOU COULD DISH OUT

Don't do what I did

Always be suspicious if your pension
adviser has a better car than you

Never take pension advice from
anyone who wants to give it to you

DAYTIME PROGRAMMES THEY SHOULD HAVE FOR RETIREES

The Great British Nod Off

———— ✦ ————

No Cash in the Attic

———— ✦ ————

Have I Got Booze for You

———— ✦ ————

Hubby's Kitchen Nightmares

DON'T DO IT! THINGS NOT TO WASTE YOUR RETIREMENT ON

Completing that 10,000-piece jigsaw
puzzle you got for Christmas

Eradicating the weeds from your
garden (it'll make the Forth Bridge
painter look like a part-timer)

Trying to discover the meaning
of life (these days it's about five
years with good behaviour)

THINGS YOUR OLD WORKMATES WILL NOW SAY TO YOU – AND YOUR REPLIES

WHAT THEY SAY...

Bet you're living the life of Riley now!

... AND YOUR REPLY

Only if Riley was an impoverished pensioner on a permanent tea break

WHAT THEY SAY...

Got your world cruise planned?

... AND YOUR REPLY

Yes, I'm still buying those lottery tickets

WHAT THEY SAY...

You lucky old so-and-so, you've escaped the rat race!

... AND YOUR REPLY

Yes, and joined the tortoise race

MYSTERIES OF RETIREMENT (PART TWO)

If you get another job and then retire again, will you have re-retired?

Why don't actors retire? Or pop stars? Or politicians? (Please…)

Do worker bees retire?

HOW, STRANGELY, YOU MIGHT BE BETTER OFF FINANCIALLY

No more taking your turn
on the cream-bun run

No more paying for work clothes, dry-
cleaning bills, season tickets, etc.

No more paying into a pension!

PURSUITS FOR BORED RETIREES (PART TWO)

A) Tot up how many hours you spent at work drinking tea, having lunch, chatting to workmates, playing computer games, looking out of the window, etc.

B) Now work out how little time you spent actually working. Shocking, isn't it?

THE ART OF DOING NOTHING

Put an important piece of paper in front of you and stare out of the window – it will be just like when you were at work!

Make a list of things you need to do. Now ignore it

Tune the TV to an empty channel – the only drawback is that you may find it more engaging than a normal channel

IF YOU EVER MISS BEING AT WORK

Put a CCTV camera outside your old workplace and watch their miserable faces as people slouch into work

Get up early on a wet Monday morning and join the rush-hour crowds – that should cure you!

Try to remember your high-fiving, heel-clicking and shouts of 'yippee' the day you finally left

JUST THINK...

If all the retirees in the UK were laid
end to end, you would have a chance of
getting a seat on the bus in the daytime

If a dog year is seven human
years then dogs should be retiring
at about the age of nine

If no one ever retired then the pensions
time bomb could be safely deactivated

PROS AND CONS

THE UPSIDE OF RETIRING...

The world is your oyster

... AND THE DOWNSIDE

The pearls are a bit thin on the ground

THE UPSIDE OF RETIRING...

You can do all those things
you always wanted to do

... AND THE DOWNSIDE

If only you could remember
what they were...

THE UPSIDE OF RETIRING...

It's an endless stretch of having nothing particular to do

... AND THE DOWNSIDE

It's an endless stretch of having nothing particular to do

SONGS YOU MIGHT
FIND YOURSELF
SINGING

'Don't Wake Me Up Before You Go-Go'

'Money's Too Tight in My Pension'

'We Have All the Time in the World'

'Working Nine to Five – Not!'

PEOPLE YOU'LL BE SEEING MORE OF NOW

The postman – mainly when he's asking you to sign for next door's parcels

People collecting for charity – but that 'I'm just a poor pensioner' routine won't cut any ice with them

Neighbours who just need 'a little favour' – have you ever wondered why so many pensioners have those security spyholes in their front doors?

BE ORIGINAL

Don't lounge around – leap around!

Don't moan like there's no tomorrow –
live like there's no tomorrow!

Don't put your feet up –
keep your chin up!

A RETIREE'S DAY

10.00 a.m. – Tumble out of bed (unless it's the weekend, when you have a lie-in)

10.30 a.m. – Have a leisurely breakfast with the papers

11.00 a.m. – Time for elevenses and tackling the crossword

1.00 p.m. – Lunch and a wee nap (have a nightmare that you're back at work)

3.00 p.m. – Have a nice cup of tea and see what's on the box

5.30 p.m. – What a load of rubbish that was. Wonder if it's too early for a drink

7.30 p.m. – Have a spot of dinner and see what else is on the box

10.30 p.m. – Go to bed after another hard day

NEW NAMES FOR YOUR HOUSE

Dungrafting

* * *

The Sunnydene Retirement Home

* * *

Bedside Manor

* * *

The Always Inn

RETIREMENT DREAMS VS PRACTICALITIES

DREAM

A little cottage by the sea

PRACTICALITY

What, and have all the relatives 'popping down' for a free holiday every other week?

DREAM

A little cottage in the country

PRACTICALITY

Ten miles to the nearest supermarket –
are you having a laugh?

DREAM

Running a lovely old country pub

PRACTICALITY

Drinking in a lovely old country
pub – now you're talking!

DREAM

Going on a world cruise

PRACTICALITY

And blow my entire pension for
a month of seasickness?

AND THE GOOD NEWS IS...

You will now never have to worry about being made redundant, being replaced by a computer or having a pay cut

You finally know what you're doing

You don't have to check with anyone else before you book your holidays

You're free! (Unless your old boss asks you back, in which case you're extremely expensive...)

GRANDPARENTING

for *Beginners*

CLIVE WHICHELOW

GRANDPARENTING FOR BEGINNERS

Clive Whichelow

£6.99
Hardback
ISBN: 978-1-84953-753-7

Just when you thought your kids were off your hands…

… along come the grandchildren. The world has changed since you had little ones of your own – you may now have to read bedtime stories from an e-book, buy designer babygrows and check all their sweets for E-numbers… welcome to grandparenting twenty-first-century style!

If you're interested in finding out more
about our books, find us on Facebook at
Summersdale Publishers and follow
us on Twitter at @Summersdale.

www.summersdale.com